Successful Facilitation in a week

SUE BROWELL

Hodder & Stoughton

A MEMBER OF THE HODDER HEADLINE GROUP

Orders: please contact Bookpoint Ltd, 39 Milton Park, Abingdon, Oxon OX14 4TD.
Telephone: (44) 01235 400414, Fax: (44) 01235 400454. Lines are open from 9.00–6.00, Monday to Saturday, with a 24 hour message answering service.
Email address: orders@bookpoint.co.uk

British Library Cataloguing in Publication Data
A catalogue record for this title is available from The British Library

ISBN 0 340 774797

First published	2000
Impression number	10 9 8 7 6 5 4 3 2 1
Year	2005 2004 2003 2002 2001 2000

Typeset by Fakenham Photosettting Limited, Fakenham, Norfolk.
Printed in Great Britain for Hodder & Stoughton Education, a division of Hodder Headline Plc, 338 Euston Road, London NW1 3BH by Cox & Wyman Ltd, Reading, Berkshire.

the Institute of Management

The Institute of Management (IM) is the leading organisation for professional management. Its purpose is to promote the art and science of management in every sector and at every level, through research, education, training and development, and representation of members' views on management issues.

This series is commissioned by IM Enterprises Limited, a subsidiary of the Institute of Management, providing commercial services.

Management House,
Cottingham Road,
Corby,
Northants NN17 1TT
Tel: 01536 204222;
Fax: 01536 201651
Website: http://www.inst-mgt.org.uk

Registered in England no 3834492
Registered office: 2 Savoy Court, Strand,
London WC2R 0EZ

CONTENTS

INTRODUCTION

Facilitation is part of the modern employee's tool kit whether they be a manager, team leader or anyone else needing to use facilitation. It is not a new skill, but more recently its value and use has increased.

Achieving successful outcomes with groups of people has never been more important. Whether the task is to solve a particular problem, to gain consensus to a course of action, to bring to the surface tensions and issues that are blocking progress, or to mediate in conflict, the process by which groups of people perform these tasks cannot be left to chance. The role of the facilitator is to design a process that will ensure a successful outcome and to gain the commitment of all those involved. Anyone working with groups to achieve change and improve effectiveness needs to be able to facilitate.

This book is intended for all those who need to facilitate work groups so that they are self-reliant, able to function effectively and independently and can find solutions to problems. The book will introduce methods that facilitators can use when working with both groups and individuals. It is relevant for those involved in facilitating organisational change, and facilitating learning and development in order that individuals and groups can improve their performance.

Those involved with facilitation need to have an understanding of the following in order to be successful. During this week we shall look at:

- When to use facilitation
- The skills of facilitation
- The role of facilitator
- Communication techniques including observation, debriefing and feedback
- Facilitating teams and groups, gaining consensus and group agreement
- Dealing with groups and difficult members
- Facilitating individuals
- Tools for the facilitator
- Benefits and disadvantages in using facilitation

Facilitation – what it's all about

Today, we will examine what facilitation is and when to use it. We will also consider learning and development for both you and the others involved in the process.

- What is facilitation?
- What is a facilitator?
- When to use facilitation
- Learning and development – you and other people

Since facilitation may not be a term with which you are familiar, let us begin by defining exactly what it is.

What is facilitation?

Facilitation is a process and a 'tool' to enable things to happen. It includes some or all of the following:

- Helping and assisting employees to achieve organisational aims and objectives
- Improving work effectiveness for both individuals and teams
- Helping to develop individuals and teams so that they find solutions to problems and are able to accept responsibility for their own work
- Helping people get their work done individually or in groups
- Helping people work together more effectively

In a nutshell, facilitation is all about improving performance and helping others to help themselves. How then, does a facilitator fit into the scheme of things?

What is a facilitator?

A facilitator is like a conductor in an orchestra. A conductor controls all the musicians but does not actually do the work of playing an instrument. Without a conductor, the musicians can still make music but the conductor creates conditions for the music to be better and more effective.

A facilitator does some or all of the following:

- Creates the right conditions for others to learn by listening, questioning, posing problems and reflecting in a supportive way
- Encourages others in order to achieve results
- Helps others to develop and maximise their skills
- Assists individuals and teams to find solutions without imposing or dictating
- Assists as and when required to speed up the process of change

It may be that you are already working as a facilitator but do not realise it! If you do some or all of the above things, then you already have some idea of what a facilitator does.

When to use facilitation

Appointing facilitators who may be managers, supervisors or line managers is one of the most effective ways of energising and accelerating business improvement. They can identify and help solve problems in the improvement process by supporting teams and individuals, and helping them to achieve lasting results more quickly and effectively. Facilitators also help communication and share best practice. In short, they are an essential component of any organisation that believes in continuous improvement.

Facilitation can be used in a number of different situations and is particularly important within organisations wishing to change and to improve performance. It can be useful when you want to:

- Improve the performance of both task and individual
- Bring about change
- Look at new approaches to learning and development
- Work with individuals
- Work with groups and teams
- Help teams reach consensus and resolve conflict
- Find ways of problem solving
- Improve motivation
- Use the consulting process
- Create successful meetings

Performance improvement

Facilitators can assist individuals and teams in identifying their strengths and weaknesses and then, via brainstorming and other techniques, demonstrate possible ways of improving performance. Facilitation can be used in appraisals with individuals, as well as with teams, to improve performance and quality.

Change

All organisations are subject to change and facilitation can help individuals and teams prepare for change and enable both individual and organisational change. It encourages greater involvement in the process of change and can help increase acceptance.

Learning and development

Facilitation techniques such as reflecting back, are useful in learning and development for individuals and groups. Facilitators are important in action learning and experiential learning (more about that later today). They can help individuals think about alternative approaches to learning and development.

Working with individuals
Facilitation is very effective on a one-to-one basis. It helps people to think about how they approach tasks, how they learn, how they perform and how they can improve their performance. It can be used as a technique in appraisals and in discussions between team leaders and team members, managers and employees.

Working with groups and teams
Facilitation aids team development and helps resolve difficulties associated with the stages of team development. Facilitators assist teams to focus on achieving tasks as well as developing the team and individuals.

Helping teams reach consensus and resolve conflict
Gaining team agreement and consensus is not always easy and sometimes conflict occurs particularly when individuals have different desires, wants, opinions and beliefs. Facilitation helps achieve consensus and resolve conflicts by ensuring that all issues and views are discussed.

Problem solving
Facilitating employees to find solutions to organisational problems encourages commitment and ownership. Employees often have realistic solutions as they are closer to some of the problems and understand the issues.

Consultancy
Internal and external consultancy is growing. Facilitation can be non-judgmental and helps clients and internal

customers identify problems and find solutions for them. This increases an acceptance of outcomes.

Improving motivation
Facilitation can improve motivation of individuals and teams in a range of different ways, for example, overcoming lack of progress, increasing involvement of employees and giving recognition for ideas.

Meetings
Effective facilitation can improve the running of meetings and outcomes. In general, individuals are encouraged to participate, decisions are made and action plans outlined and agreed upon. Before facilitation begins, particularly in groups, certain ground rules should be established and individuals should get to know each other. In addition, for facilitation to be successful, the organisation needs to have other supportive systems and structures in place, for example 'no blame' culture, employees empowered to make decisions, team working.

So, before the group meets, make sure that you

- Establish ground rules, for example, confidentiality, not using mobile phones, not interrupting other people, not criticising ideas
- Check that people know each other: share names, position, job responsibilities and any other relevant information that individuals are willing to share
- Arrange the layout of room – a circular or semi-circular shape helps facilitation as no one is seen to be in charge
- Have an agenda/programme

Learning and development

Facilitators are important in action learning and experiential learning because they can help individuals think about alternative approaches to learning and development.

Action learning
Traditionally, we learn something and then try to apply it to a situation. Action learning means that we start working on a real project, problem or issue and, in doing so, learn key skills. Typically, teams work on organisational problems/issues with a facilitator to find solutions. The facilitator ensures effective group working.

The key factors in action learning are that it:

- Increases the process of learning from experience
- Enables people to learn from their own experiences
- Solves problems within organisations
- Can bring about organisational change and development

- Is based on the team/group
- Is concerned with developing skills
- Is work-based, using organisational problems/issues
- Is focused on workplace outcomes
- Is employee-centred
- Uses a facilitator and not a teacher/trainer

Use action learning now to find out more about facilitation and improve your facilitation skills, as well as being a facilitator for others using action learning.

Experiential learning
Experiential learning is based on learning through real experience, using observation and reflection, thinking of new approaches and then trying them out. Throughout, the individual is aware of the learning that is taking place. Facilitators help individuals and teams learn from experience and increase awareness of learning. When you facilitate, encourage others actively to get involved: take action, review the experience, learn from the experience and then practice.

Ask yourself:

- What problem/project can I get involved in where I can start to use facilitation skills?
- What can I learn from it so far?
- What do I want to do now?
- What is the best way of going about this?

Setting personal objectives is important in helping you to learn new skills and to develop. Some of the personal objectives you might consider as part of action learning include:

- Understanding of facilitation and facilitation techniques
- Understanding the role of facilitator and the skills needed to be a good facilitator
- Developing the team and enabling them to find solutions
- Encouraging others to accept responsibility
- Gaining more participation
- Solving problems together
- Becoming a guide – helping rather than telling
- Being an advisor rather than a leader
- Helping others help themselves
- Assessing and reinforcing existing facilitation skills
- Using facilitation at work to make life easier
- Working with other facilitators to facilitate events
- Being personally more effective

So start thinking about your personal objectives now. By the end of this book you should have a greater understanding of:

- The role of facilitator and facilitation skills to achieve optimum results
- The use of facilitation tools, including problem-solving tools
- The selection and use of facilitation methods and techniques to meet the needs of individuals and groups
- How to help resolve difficulties during group activities and deal with unhelpful behaviour
- The use of facilitation techniques as a means of helping group members improve their performance
- Facilitation in learning and development
- Effective debriefing and feedback
- Co-facilitation

Summary

So, today we learnt what facilitation is about, what facilitators do and when to use it. We know that:

- Facilitation is about helping others help themselves to improve and accept responsibility
- Facilitators are like a conductor or a catalyst to speed up the process and make it easier
- Facilitation can be used in many different situations
- Learning and development is important in facilitation and is associated with action

Skills of facilitation

Today, we will examine the skills needed to be an effective facilitator. We will also consider the role of a facilitator and facilitator style.

- The skills of facilitation
- The role of a facilitator
- Facilitator style

Skills of the facilitator

Managers, team leaders and others who want to facilitate need a range of different skills to maximise their effectiveness. In particular, they need excellent communication, non-verbal communication and questioning techniques, as well as skills such as decision-making, an understanding of group dynamics and the ability to develop teams. Personal skills such as tolerance, patience and knowing when to intervene are also important. You may already possess some or all of the skills associated with facilitation but may not have used them consciously for facilitating individuals and groups. The key skills of a successful facilitator are:

- Listening skills
- Questioning techniques
- Paraphrasing and restatement
- Summarising
- Ability to maintain silence
- Non-verbal communication
- Consensus and group agreement
- Observation
- Understanding individuals
- Understanding group dynamics and team development
- Debriefing and constructive feedback

Think about the skills that you already have as well as those you currently do not possess. We shall be looking at many of the skills required in more detail throughout this week.

Listening skills

These are one of the most important facilitation skills. You must show you are actively listening by your body language and responses. Lean forward, make eye contact and acknowledge what others are saying by affirmative head-nodding, appropriate facial expressions and use of silence. Ensure the setting helps the listening process by being non-threatening, conducive to conversation and, when necessary, private. Listening skills are needed for good management and in most relationships.

Questioning techniques
You need to ask questions that will help the individual or group focus on achieving the task, learn and develop and think about what they are doing. Use open questions that encourage the individual to talk. Probe questions allow a more in-depth investigation whilst closed questions provide simple yes or no answers and are not always helpful. Link questions allow the facilitator to connect topics without having to jump from subject to subject. Comparison questions allow individuals to make a choice, whilst hypothetical questions allow individuals to think about new ideas. They can also help the facilitator to check an individual's knowledge.

Paraphrasing and restatement
This puts what the person said into your own words without changing the basic meaning. Paraphrasing shows that you are listening and understanding what the individual is saying. Restatement goes beyond paraphrasing because it provides a preliminary interpretation of the situation. It helps you to check out what you believe might be happening with the individual and the situation.

Summarising
Summarising what is happening is useful for both you as facilitator and the individual or group. It shows that you have listened and understood but it can also help in making decisions and assist others in moving forward. Getting team members to arrive at their own summaries and conclusions is very useful. It shows that they have fully understood all

the issues before reaching decisions. It also enables them to take 'ownership' of the process and the decision.

Ability to maintain silence
Maintaining silence demonstrates effective listening and gives an individual time to think. Be patient, maintain self-control and eye contact and demonstrate interest. Encourage people to take their time.

Non-verbal communication
Facilitators should be aware of the non-verbal messages they are giving individuals and the non-verbal messages they receive in return. It is possible for both parties to make assumptions and misinterpretations based on non-verbal messages and dress, jewellery, hair, touch, body space, eye contact, etc.

Consensus and group agreement
Facilitators need to be able to help others generate ideas via brainstorming and then obtain consensus and commitment to an action or decision by allowing time to discuss issues and form conclusions. They need to deal with

disagreements and, when necessary, work towards a compromise so that action is agreed with the full approval of the group or team.

Observation
Facilitators need to be able to observe individuals, groups and teams accurately in order to understand what is happening.

Understanding individuals
As a facilitator, you need to understand individual differences in personality, ability, attitudes and how people behave in groups and teams. Sometimes you will need to bring together individuals to resolve conflict or communication difficulties and you need to understand why such difficulties occur. You will also need to facilitate learning and development for individuals and be able to recognise individual potential.

Understanding group dynamics and team development
Understanding individual differences helps to understand group dynamics and group processes. Facilitators must manage conflict and deal with individuals whose behaviour hinders the group process. Skilled facilitators use the group itself to resolve difficulties. An effective facilitator ensures that the task is achieved and the team is developed by creating a teamwork culture, and encouraging open communication, problem solving and team decision making. Developing the team encourages team accountability and the resolution of problems.

Debriefing and constructive feedback
Debriefing reinforces what happened, resolves misunderstandings and clarifies why things occurred.

Constructive feedback provides individuals and groups with the opportunity to learn, develop and improve. Start with a positive approach, be specific and refer only to those things that can be changed. Avoid personal attacks and be objective at all times.

Other skills
Facilitators need to be open and develop trust. You must be tolerant, patient and remain neutral – for much of the time you will have a back-seat role. You need to be an advisor rather than a leader and encourage others to accept responsibility, yet you must recognise when you need to intervene. You therefore also need to have influencing skills, be able to run meetings, understand and be able to set objectives, plan effectively and determine problems by assessing a situation. You also need good presentation skills to help summarise ideas and suggestions. Other skills of an effective facilitator include time management, the ability to use a range of tools and methods such as brainstorming, discussion techniques and the provision of support and encouragement.

The role of a facilitator

At work your role may change. At different times you might be a leader, a manager or a facilitator. It is quite possible to use any of these roles depending upon the issue, situation or problem but the three roles are very different and must not be confused. If you are a leader or a manager you will probably take control of situations and direct people. However, you need also to remember that facilitators are there to support and help people and organisations but not to do or to implement. The facilitating role is basically that of observer, supporter, listener and helper. The role of facilitators is principally to help:

- People achieve things – solve problems and make decisions
- Individuals (particularly in a team) discuss their views
- People think of new ideas and communicate them to others

- All team members to participate and reach consensus
- People perform well
- People develop as individuals and within teams
- The organisation develop by exploring new ideas through its people
- Individuals and teams cope with change

There are some essential 'dos' and 'don'ts' associated with the role of a facilitator.

Do	Don't
Ensure that the group concentrates on achieving the task	Take control and start implementing and 'doing'
Ensure the group is working to achieve its objective(s)	Take the lead
Ensure open discussion and decision-making within groups and with individuals	Contribute your ideas and views
Encourage all team members to make a contribution	Tell group members what to do
Help the group solve problems by using a variety of methods	Criticise and be negative
Protect individuals and their ideas from attack particularly within groups	Make decisions
Help people find solutions that they are happy with both individually and within groups	Feel that you are losing status and control. An effective facilitator is also an effective manager/team leader and a valuable employee

Facilitator style

The style of each facilitator is unique, depending on that individual's personality and personal skills. The style of a facilitator is not authoritarian, rather it emphasises trust, innovation and risk-taking, particularly when working in teams to achieve improved productivity, performance and quality. Your style will develop over time and will reflect your own personality and values, your experience and the training and development in facilitation that you undertake. However, the skills needed for effective facilitation are often found in the best managers and team leaders even if they are not always used for facilitation.

Case history

Simon is a manager who uses facilitation skills, developed over a period of time, as part of his job. When he joined the organisation, he appreciated the usefulness of his boss's facilitation skills, so when Simon was promoted to team leader, he developed his own facilitation skills and continues to do so now he has reached management level.

As manager, Simon has organisational objectives to achieve, together with his staff. He is particularly concerned with quality and performance improvement. His staff work in teams and he meets regularly with them to facilitate team meetings, encouraging all staff to contribute ideas and communicate both with each other and with other teams. He listens and asks questions but leaves the decision-making to the individuals and teams. Sometimes this is a difficult task. On the one hand it is tempting to simply tell them what to do; but on the other hand, his staff often have better solutions than him to problems. He understands the importance of allowing his staff to think for themselves as this is the most positive way to find solutions. When staff criticise systems and the organisation he helps them to channel their complaints constructively in order to make the changes required.

He understands that all staff should have the opportunity to speak. One way to do this is to write down suggestions on a flip chart to provide a focus for discussion and help summarise what has been said. By asking useful and helpful questions to get his staff thinking and to explore further options, but not putting forward suggestions himself, he helps to bring out all the issues and turn the situation into something constructive with positive, rather than destructive and negative, outcomes.

Whether he works with individuals on a one-to-one basis, or with teams, Simon's goal is to develop his staff and improve their performance. He is concerned that all his staff continually learn and develop.

What are your own skills?

You need to review your skills and level of competence regularly so that you, too, can develop and improve. Think about the skills you already have, and those you can develop.

- Which facilitation skills do you already possess?
- How good are your existing skills and how can you improve your level of competence?
- Which facilitation skills are absent from your tool box of skills?
- Which facilitation skills do you need to develop and how will you do this?

Summary

Today we have learnt about the skills of facilitation, the role of a facilitator and facilitator style:

- Facilitators need a range of different skills to be effective
- Many skills needed for facilitation are used in everyday situations, for example, communication, working with teams and personal skills such as tolerance and decision-making
- The role of a facilitator is to help other people develop, achieve things and improve their performance
- The style of a facilitator will vary as everyone is unique

Communication techniques

Today, we examine communication techniques for effective facilitation. We will also consider the skills of observation, debriefing and feedback.

- Communication techniques
- Observation
- Debriefing

Communication techniques

Communication techniques are vitally important for effective facilitation, so you will need to develop:

- Listening skills
- The use of appropriate questions
- Paraphrasing and restatement
- Non verbal skills
- Observation
- Debriefing and feedback

It is important to try and assess how good your communication skills are.

There are a number of tests and assessments you can use but the simplest one is to ask those people with whom you work and have contact, such as colleagues, supervisors, administrative staff – even your partner – for honest and constructive feedback. Think carefully about whom to ask. Not everyone can be brutally frank; you need an opinion that you can trust – even if you don't like everything you hear! As we said yesterday, it is vital to review and assess your skills regularly and, as a result, develop and improve them further.

Listening skills

Listening is probably the single most important skill for effective facilitation. Show that you are listening by your body language and responses. Lean forward, make eye contact and acknowledge what others are saying. Listening skills can be divided into a number of different areas:

- Non-verbal
- Verbal
- Finding the appropriate setting
- Understanding the barriers to good listening

Non-verbal skills

Eye contact is one way of communicating full and undivided attention whilst listening. It can easily be achieved by focusing your eyes on the other person, while occasionally moving your gaze away from the person to avoid staring. Staring can be seen as hostile and tends to raise anxiety levels. However, avoid looking away from the person for long periods of time as this might be interpreted as a lack of interest. In short, be natural.

Other important non-verbal aspects of listening include affirmative head nodding. Head nods demonstrate that you are listening and are particularly encouraging when used with eye contact. Appropriate facial expressions are also effective. Silence is another important aspect of listening as it communicates patience and gives the person time to think through the reply to a question. Finally, try to maintain an open body posture as this helps the other person to relax, be less defensive and talk more freely. Do this by facing the person rather than sitting or standing at his or her side. Ensure that your arms and legs are uncrossed as crossed arms and legs can communicate superiority or defensiveness as well as serving as a barrier. Lean forward slightly as this communicates interest, but don't overdo it – slouching is an indication of boredom, tiredness or lack of interest.

Verbal skills
The facilitator sometimes needs to encourage the other person to open up, examine their thoughts and discuss issues through verbal prompts. Such verbal prompts show that the facilitator is actively listening. These prompts encourage the person to talk. Expressions such as *Um-hum, Ye-s, Go on, I see, Can you tell me some more about that*? are very effective prompts, as is repeating key words. For example, if the person says, *I don't know, I guess I'm just confused,* the facilitator repeats the word *confused*? This prompts the person to say more. Asking a variety of

questions also helps the person to focus on issues, as well as clarifying certain things for the facilitator.

Choosing the setting
The setting in which the listening takes place can obviously help or hinder the process. Technically, listening can take place anywhere, but ideally choose a place that is non-threatening and conducive to conversation in order to put the person at ease. As far as possible, try to ensure an atmosphere of privacy; distractions such as phone calls, people walking in on you, other people within earshot, should be minimised. Close the door and divert phone calls to show that you are giving your full attention. Making an effort to ensure privacy shows the other person that you are really interested. A large desk between you and the person can be a psychological as well as a physical barrier. It says, 'I'm still superior to you and I reserve the right to pass judgement on you.' Create a climate that stresses the equality of your relationship, by sitting at the same level as the person, with no desks between you.

Avoiding barriers to good listening

No matter how difficult the situation, do give the other person your complete attention. Knowing what some of the barriers to good listening are, and an awareness of how to avoid them, will help you to listen more effectively. Avoid 'on-off' listening which arises from the fact that most of us think about four times as fast as the average person speaks. The listener therefore has ¾ of a minute of spare thinking time for each listening minute and can use this to think about other things. Sometimes we get upset or irritated when we hear certain words or topics and stop listening. Try not to let personal dislikes, views and prejudices get in the way, or to jump to conclusions. Sometimes we decide quickly that either the subject or the speaker is boring and stop listening. Avoid day dreaming whilst apparently listening as the other person will realise that you are not listening. Remember to concentrate on the person and not the problem. Try not to remember all the facts or even write them down as you will miss some things as the person keeps on talking. Finally, try to reduce the number of distractions such as background noise or movement of people as this interferes with effective listening.

Developing your listening skills
Reviewing your listening skills can help identify areas that need developing. Ask others for feedback on existing skills, formulate an action plan for improvement and then ask for feedback on your progress. Key questions to think about are:

- Do you show interest in the person speaking?
- Do you allow prejudices and emotions to get in the way?
- Do you show interest in the subject under discussion even when it is boring?
- Do you avoid being critical of the other person?
- Do you check for understanding and summarise what is said?
- Do you create the right environment for listening?
- Are you patient and tolerant?
- Do you allow time for the person to discuss issues?

The use of questions

Asking questions is important for many different reasons. It shows that you are listening, it helps clarify certain issues, and it assists the person to explore options and to discuss and describe them effectively. There are many different types of questions.

Open questions
These are particularly useful questions as they encourage the individual to talk, for example, *Tell me about ... , Describe to me how ... , Explain to me how ... , How do you feel about ... ? What importance does this have in relation to ... ?*

Probe questions
These follow on from open questions and allow more in-depth investigation, for example, *What did you learn from that experience? What was the most difficult part? Better in what ways? Why do you think...? Why was that? Can you give me an example?* However, take care not to ask too many probe questions as it can easily become an 'interrogation' and appear critical or blaming. You need to think about how many probe questions you should ask.

Closed questions
Since these encourage 'yes' or 'no' answers, they are not always particularly useful, for example, *Do you think the project you are working on is too difficult ... ? Is it true that ... ? Do you think that ... ? Would you agree that ... ? Were you responsible for ... ?*

Link questions
These allow the facilitator to link topics without having to jump from subject to subject, for example, *You mentioned that it is difficult to find the time for all that has to be done. What are your views on delegation?*

Leading questions
These usually result in a person giving a reply that pleases the questioner so are not very useful, for example, *Don't you think that the attitude of younger staff today leaves much to be desired? I suppose you found that boring?*

Evaluative questions
These often allow the facilitator to give his/her opinion with regard to a person's statement and does not encourage further discussion, for example, *Don't you think that was rather hasty? Surely you don't think that will work?* It would be much

better to use an open question such as, *Faced with similar circumstances again, what action would you take?*

Comparison questions
These allow the person to give a preference or choice if the alternatives are fair, for example, *Do you enjoy working with people or do you prefer administrative work?*

Hypothetical questions
These allow the person to think about new ideas or allow the facilitator to check on individuals' knowledge, for example, *What would you do if . . . ?*

Multiple questions
A string of questions one after another serves no useful purpose at all, for example, *When you started this job did you realise the pace at which you would have to work? Do you find it difficult to keep up to date? How does this compare with your previous job?* Definitely a technique to be avoided!

Playback questions
A playback is when a facilitator repeats a key word that they have heard during the course of the conversation. For example, if the person says, *I thought that was the correct approach but maybe I misunderstood*, the facilitator repeats the word *misunderstood*? This then prompts the person to say more without you using a long question that might interrupt that person's thinking.

Clarifying questions
Questions such as, *How do you feel about it? Can you give me an example?* and *What does this mean to you?* help focus the person's attention on certain issues and provide clarification for the facilitator.

Focusing questions
Often in the early stages of facilitation, the person may discuss several different subjects. The facilitator may then ask a question to help focus the discussions, for example, *Which is the most important thing that we've talked about in the last ten minutes?*

Paraphrasing and restatement

The purpose of paraphrasing is to show that you are listening to and comprehend what the individual is saying. Do this by putting what the person said into your own words without changing the basic meaning. For example, the person states, *I'm frustrated that I don't have direct control over some of the people working on this project. It can affect my success with it.* The facilitator can respond by saying, *You're concerned that your success might be affected by the quality of work of people you don't manage.*

Restatement goes further than paraphrasing because it includes some simple, preliminary interpretation of the situation. The purpose of restatement is to check out what you believe might be occurring with the person. So, if the person says, *So far, I've been able to persuade supervisors to give their people good feedback, but I may not always be able to do that,* the facilitator may then ask, *You feel that one area of control you have over these people is diminishing?*

Non-verbal skills

The facilitator should be aware of non-verbal messages from the person such as facial expression and body posture, and also that individuals may well be picking up non-verbal messages from the facilitator. If people are smiling, nodding, leaning forward and/or maintaining eye contact they are feeling enthusiastic, interested and agreeing with what is happening. If they are yawning, looking away, leaning backwards, shuffling feet, looking at the clock, then they are bored, tired or uninterested. If they are frowning, scratching their head, staring into space and avoiding eye contact, they may be feeling confused or disagreeing or suppressing feelings. It is possible for both parties to make assumptions, judgements and misinterpretations based on non-verbal messages, including style of dress, jewellery, hair and make-up. It is particularly important to consider culture and ethnic groups in terms of body language and non-verbal communication, as it is quite possible to make unfair assumptions.

Observation

Observing effectively is an important communication skill for facilitators, and like any other skill needs to be developed and practised in order to become competent. Sometimes facilitators will record their observations, particularly if they are working with a group or team. Observations can be recorded in a number of different ways such as a narrative or descriptive account of what has been seen. Critical incidents can be recorded in terms of significant moments, demonstration of certain behaviour and specific events. Particular behaviours and characteristics within groups/teams can be recorded as well as those of individuals.

Remember, when you are observing, to focus on actual events and behaviours; do not interpret, make judgements or record your perceptions of what happened. It is sometimes helpful to divide what you see into non-verbal and verbal examples. Non-verbal examples include facial expressions, gestures, body postures and personal space; verbal examples include information giving, information seeking, proposing, supporting, tension release, wandering, disagreeing and attacking. Write these headings on an observation sheet to help you record your observations.

Avoid being drawn into discussions and debates as this reduces your ability to observe objectively. Your role is to observe, not take part.

Use meetings, discussions, briefings, or any other time where there is human interaction, in order to develop and polish your observation skills.

Debriefing

Debriefing skills are important for the facilitator in a range of different situations such as learning and development, group and team formation and team development. Debriefing can be used immediately after an activity or exercise and should:

- Reinforce what actually happened
- Clear up any misunderstandings
- Work out why things occurred
- Highlight feelings of all involved
- Provide an opportunity for self-observation
- Provide ways of understanding interaction
- Provide an opportunity for suggestions and criticisms
- Relate activity to other situations
- Tie up loose ends

Feedback

In general terms, feedback should be on an individual basis, although there will be cases relating to teams and training events when more open and collective feedback is appropriate. Constructive feedback increases self-awareness, offers options and encourages development. It does not need to be purely positive; negative feedback given skilfully can also be very important and useful. Negative feedback is not the same as destructive feedback, which leaves the recipient with nothing on which to build or without options for using the learning. Useful feedback is a way of learning more about ourselves as facilitators and the effect our behaviour has on others. It is important to learn to both give and receive feedback. Use the following guidelines when giving feedback.

Start with the positive

Most people need encouragement and to be told when they are doing something well. If the positive is registered first, any negative feedback is more likely to be listened to and acted upon. Provide balanced feedback – comment on things which an individual has done well and should continue to do, as well as areas for improvement.

Be specific
Try to avoid general comments that are not very useful when it comes to developing skills. Statements such as *You were brilliant* or *You were awful* may be encouraging or dreadful to hear but they do not give enough detail to be useful sources of learning. Specific feedback relating to behaviour and events gives more opportunity for learning.

Refer only to behaviour that can be changed
It is not helpful to give a person feedback about something over which they have no choice or control, for example a stammer or nervous twitch. On the other hand to be told that *It would help me if you looked at me when you speak* can give the person something to develop and improve upon.

Provide alternatives
If you do offer negative feedback, do not simply criticise but suggest what the person could have done differently or help them to explore alternatives. Turn the negative into an opportunity for improvement.

Be descriptive rather than evaluative
Tell the person what you saw or heard and the effect it had rather than stating something was 'good' or 'bad'. For example, *Your tone of voice as you said that really made me feel that you were concerned* is likely to be more useful than, *That was good*.

Leave the recipient with a choice
Feedback that demands change or is imposed heavily on the other person may encourage resistance. Skilled feedback offers people information about themselves in a way that leaves them with a choice about whether or not to do anything.

Provide feedback on behaviour that has been observed
Give feedback based on what you saw the person doing, rather than what you thought they were thinking or intending.

Ask questions rather than make statements
In this way, individuals can begin to analyse their own behaviour and reflect. For example, *How else could you have reacted when ... ?* is more thought-provoking than, *You should have ....*

Consider value to the individual
In general, feedback should be confidential and between the individual and facilitator only. It should have value to the individual so that they can change and improve. If not, there is little value in providing feedback. Limit feedback to the most important issues. Providing too much feedback is not helpful as individuals can not change habits overnight.

Think what the feedback says about you
Giving feedback is a two-way process and says a great deal about your values and what you focus on in others. Therefore you can learn about yourself from the feedback you give others.

Consider how skilled at feedback you are and get opinions on your skills from friends, family, partner, colleagues, managers and others at work. Review your skills and devise an action plan for development and improvement. Ask yourself: *How easy do I find it to give feedback?* and *How easy do I find it to receive feedback?* Almost always, sometimes, almost never?

Summary

So now we know something about communication techniques, observation, debriefing and feedback:

- Communication techniques are vitally important for facilitation and include listening skills, questioning techniques and non-verbal communication
- Facilitators need to be able to observe individuals within groups and teams so they can understand group dynamics and what is happening
- Facilitators need to be able to help others understand what has happened during an event by debriefing them
- Facilitators need to be able to both give and receive feedback, so that learning and improvement can occur for everyone

Up to now, we have discussed the skills required of a facilitator. Tomorrow we shall begin to put them into action.

Facilitating teams and groups

Today, we will examine what is needed to facilitate teams and groups, particularly in meetings. We will also look at how to deal with difficult group members and achieve consensus and group agreement.

- Facilitating teams and groups
- Meetings
- Dealing with groups and difficult members
- Consensus and group agreement

Facilitating teams and groups

Within organisations there are several tasks and objectives to achieve. Using facilitation is a way of ensuring that those tasks and objectives are met. Group and team working are common within organisations. The facilitator will often work with groups and teams to explore and diagnose problems or clarify tasks, and then help them to find and implement solutions for themselves. Effective group problem-solving is a critical success factor for many organisations. Facilitators must therefore have an understanding of team development, group dynamics and conflict in order that they can be effective. Their role is similar to that of a cox of a rowing team. In order to achieve maximum speed – and success – the cox must ensure that the crew are working together in harmony for the same goal.

Team development

Teams tend to go through various stages before they become fully effective. A facilitator needs to recognise the different stages, observe group behaviour and help the team move from one stage to another.

Stage 1

The first stage is when individuals come together for the first time to form a team. Team members are often hesitant, suspicious and looking for a sense of belonging whilst closely watching other team members' behaviour. The facilitator needs to ensure that team members get acquainted and are sensitive to other people's needs. The facilitator also needs to encourage team-building and awareness.

Stage 2

Stage 2 occurs when individuals begin to exert their individual strengths and weaknesses without performing effectively. There is often conflict between team members together with concern over individual responsibilities and team member roles. The facilitator needs to be positive and to deal with conflict openly, reassuring the team that conflict is normal. The team needs to be given more responsibility and increased awareness of team-building.

Stage 3
Now the team begins to come together, conflict is reduced and the team starts to perform more effectively. Team members tend to rely significantly on the facilitator, but there is more obvious team cohesion and reduced conflict. The facilitator tries to reduce dependence, and encourage greater team responsibility and team development.

Stage 4
Finally, the team matures and is self-functioning. It is able to solve difficult issues and this is reflected in terms of high performance. The team members are loyal to each other and are confident. The team is competitive with other teams and has a need for more information and more innovation. The facilitator continues to train and develop the team, encouraging team members to change roles in an environment of trust and commitment. The facilitator's involvement in the team is reduced.

The role of the facilitator in team development is crucial in:

- Consistently supporting and challenging the team to take greater levels of responsibility within their roles
- Maintaining team focus, building teams and focusing on how the team is working together
- Helping the team to arrive at an agreed set of rules for the ways in which it will work

- Encouraging team members to determine their own issues for discussion and encouraging full participation by all team members
- Using the members of the team productively in arriving at positive and creative solutions
- Seeing members of the team as individuals, recognising particular traits, strengths and weaknesses
- Helping the group when it is unable to proceed
- Encouraging team problem-solving and decision-making
- Preparing groups for change
- Relating organisational objectives to the process of facilitating teams to meet those objectives and helping people from different disciplines or from different parts of the organisation to work together

Working with a group

As well as developing the team, the facilitator needs to ensure that individual members are developed and that the task is achieved. The facilitator needs to identify what is required before, during and after a group session.

Before a group session the facilitator will:

1. Organise equipment, rooms and furniture, and ensure that there will be no distractions or interruptions.
2. Consider the implications of time of day, place, and room layout on the team and task.
3. Acquire background information and define objectives for their own purposes whilst recognising that the group has its objectives.

4. Choose a range of methods appropriate for the task and the group and consider the size and composition of sub-groups.
5. Plan procedures that will involve all participants and then balance the task with an individual's needs.
6. Spend time with individuals where appropriate.

During a group session the facilitator will:

1. Ensure that ground rules and boundaries are established regarding communication, decision-making and way of working.
2. Ensure that tasks are clarified and the group focuses on the task; from time to time check understanding and summarise progress; towards the end check what has been achieved and that action plans have been identified.
3. Behave in a way that conveys respect, trust, understanding and genuineness.
4. Listen, bring in group members to ensure active participation and ask questions.
5. Provide encouragement, support and feedback, with contributions being positively accepted and built upon.
6. Manage conflict and deal with difficult members appropriately.
7. At the end, ask how the session might have been better and help identify areas for improvement.

After a group session the facilitator will:

1. Review achievements and learning both personally and for the group, establishing the learning that can be applied in the future.
2. Provide feedback, particularly recognition of achievement.
3. Provide specific follow-up with individuals who need support and further development should be highlighted.

Remember that group sizes vary – sometimes you may be working with large groups, and sometimes with small groups or sub-groups. You may need to alter or adjust your way of working.

Meetings

Some of the issues associated with groups and teams can also be found in meetings. Meetings can take various forms and may not necessarily comprise groups or teams but a collection of individuals. However, the processes such as room layout, establishing ground rules, ensuring that all participants know each other, recording information, managing time and group dynamics can be very similar. Therefore the facilitator needs to use a variety of facilitation skills and methods. Meetings are a particular form of group working and individual personalities may be evident with the possibility of conflict, so you will need to know how to cope with difficult individuals.

Dealing with groups and difficult members

The facilitator may experience difficulties in working with groups particularly in the form of conflict and difficult individual members. Conflict arises when people appear to have different desires, wants, opinions and beliefs. Ask the following questions to help groups work through conflict:

- What is the issue or problem?
- Where do we not agree?
  Areas of disagreement must be identified so they can be dealt with as separate issues or problems to be resolved.
- Where do we agree?
  Where there are areas of agreement, they should be built upon.
- What action(s) will we take as the next step to resolve the conflict?
  Actions represent what each individual will do as a result of the discussion and should specify the action, the name of the person responsible and the completion date.

Remember when you are dealing with groups to avoid verbally attacking individuals within them. Wherever possible, use control from within the group. Here are some guidelines for recognising types of people, whose behaviour can create difficulty in groups, and options for managing them.

The non-participator

This type of person may be reluctant to participate for a number of reasons, so try to establish what the reasons are on a one-to-one basis. Warn the group, *In a few minutes I shall ask for suggestions*, and then ask for everyone's views individually. Look for active participation and encourage and praise any involvement. Give the individual a special job or task, for example, observer or note-taker, and place with a friendly sub-group to work. Keep the subject matter varied and relevant to the individual and, where possible, allow them to choose task. Give time and be patient but challenge where appropriate. Ensure that the group are aware that success is as much their responsibility as yours, and work on relationships within the group.

The non-talker

It is important to establish the reason for the silence. Place the non-talker in a small sub-group with supportive friends. Provide support, reward any contributions and praise involvement. Protect the person from verbal attack by other group members. Where possible, involve the person by asking simple direct questions and questions which they will feel confident to answer to increase self-confidence. Find a topic that interests the person and give time for its preparation. Be patient and take the opportunity to observe the group and measure the contributions of all group members. Encourage the individual outside the group, giving feedback on a one-to-one basis. Consider using role-plays for the individual to build up skills if necessary.

The talker, know-all, dominant type

The facilitator needs to avoid eye contact and direct questions away from them. Acknowledge their contribution but interrupt tactfully to allow other members to speak. Place in a sub-group with other similar types. Allocate the talker a specific task for example, recording group findings that does not involve talking. Try to limit the person's speaking time and, if necessary, record contribution levels of all group members to ensure that time is shared equally. Ask opinions and bring in other members to ensure that no one individual monopolises the situation. Develop assertiveness in other group members.

The bully, aggressive type

Seek the causes of aggression and bullying, and try to remove them. Give feedback to the individual via a private confidential chat. Establish appropriate ground rules for group working before beginning, and encourage the group to apply sanctions for aggressive behaviour. Confront aggressive behaviour when it happens and reinforce acceptable behaviour. Keep the person physically close to you and away from any particular targets. Hold back his/her contribution until others have had their say to prevent them exerting an undue influence on the discussion. If all else fails, exclude the person from the group and discuss their behaviour outside the group. Develop assertiveness skills to replace aggressive behaviour by one-to-one coaching and development, or a training course.

The joker

Discuss with the group the use and misuse of humour. Establish rules for group working and use the group to provide sanctions. Give feedback on the disruptive effects of their behaviour and allow time for change. Do not allow the person an audience and keep close to you where they can be supervised. Encourage acceptable behaviour and, if necessary, provide further feedback and follow-up outside the group on appropriate behaviour.

The quarrelsome type
Do not be drawn into arguments. Ask for comments from other strong members of the group to exert control. Stop them monopolising the meeting by bringing in other group members. Emphasise the need for constructive comments.

The unco-operative, 'rejecting' type
Establish appropriate ground rules and give responsibility to the group for dealing with the behaviour. Confront the behaviour when it happens and support/reinforce acceptable behaviour. Emphasise the need for constructive comments and provide feedback on behaviour. Allow group members to choose whom to work with.

The thick-skinned, uninterested type
Ask the person for contributions in areas where you know they are interested or have detailed knowledge. Encourage their efforts and show how decisions will affect them personally.

The highbrow type
Protect the person from verbal attack. Keep them involved but emphasise the need for practical solutions, encouraging them to talk in terms of what must actually be done.

The misfit/loner
Give feedback as appropriate. Accept the person by supporting and encouraging. Create an opportunity for achievement and give special encouragement. Allocate a special role or responsibility. Develop sensitivity in other group members and encourage group responsibility.

At the end of the day, you need to consider for whom in the group the difficult member is a problem:

- Is the person a problem for you as facilitator?
- Is the person a problem for group members?
- Is the person a problem in achieving the group task?
- Is the person causing problems for themselves?

When you have identified the problem:

- Consider what you would like to change and how this can be done
- Investigate the reasons for the unacceptable behaviour and consider the different strategies to help change or control the situation
- Consider whether your own behaviour or that of the group needs changing

Consensus and group agreement

Consensus is important when facilitators work with groups although there may be disagreements and conflicts before agreement is finally achieved. Consensus is achieved when individual team members can answer 'yes' to the following types of questions:

- Do you agree that this is the next stage?
- Can you work with this?
- Are you happy with this course of action?
- Now that all issues have been discussed, can we progress?

It is unlikely that all group members will agree with all outcomes and actions. What is important, is that they can support the decisions made. The facilitator should be instrumental in obtaining consensus and this can be achieved by:

- Establishing criteria
- Allowing time to discuss issues and form conclusions
- Expecting and dealing with conflict
- Being prepared to negotiate and collaborate
- Establishing facts
- Ensuring that facts are more important than opinions
- Using structured decision-making tools
- Encouraging group members to discuss issues and not to avoid conflict

If difficulties do occur, then the facilitator can:

- Allow members to disagree – 'agree to disagree'
- Take time out or defer the issue to a later time
- Work towards a compromise

The facilitator should try to work towards a win–win situation as a win–lose situation is only a short-term strategy. One team or a part of the team may win in the short term, but you must take into account the important long-term implications in terms of trust, working practices and relationships both within the organisation and externally.

Summary

Today we learnt about facilitating teams and groups, meetings, dealing with groups and difficult members and achieving consensus and group agreement.

- Facilitators need to understand the stages of team development and their role in the process
- Effective facilitators need to prepare before a group session, work with a group and follow-up after the group session
- There are similarities between team and group events, and meetings, and many of the same principles can be applied to meetings
- Facilitators need to recognise conflict within groups and help groups resolve the conflict
- Groups and teams comprise many different individuals – facilitators need to understand different

behaviours and have strategies for dealing with such difficulties
- Facilitators have an important role in helping groups and teams achieve consensus and group agreement

Tomorrow we examine the individual.

Facilitating individuals and the tools required

Today, we will take a look at how to facilitate individuals and the importance of objective setting in facilitation. We will also consider the tools that can be used for successful facilitation.

- Facilitating individuals
- Objective setting
- Tools for the facilitator

Facilitating individuals

Facilitation is as effective on a one-to-one basis as for groups and teams. Many of the principles outlined earlier this week, apply equally to individuals and groups. Facilitators need to understand how to deal effectively with difficult members not only within a group but also on an individual basis. On a more positive note, facilitation helps individuals think about how they approach tasks and achieve success. Facilitation can be used to assist individual learning and development and for improving performance. It is a useful technique in appraisals and in discussions between team leaders and team members, managers and employees for a variety of different purposes. The facilitator can assist the individual in their preparation for change, in improving motivation and in overcoming individual difficulties.

Objective setting

As part of their work, facilitators need to be able to set objectives both for themselves and for others. Their own objectives may not be explicit but unless they know what they want to achieve or what they want a group to achieve, they will be unable to ensure that the appropriate decisions are made and action taken. Such objectives are essential to ensure that individuals and groups continue working towards completing tasks on time and achieving success.

An objective is simply a statement outlining something to be achieved in the future without describing how to get there. Facilitators must have some understanding of what has to be achieved; however, they need individuals and teams to provide the precise details of how to fulfil those objectives and provide the resources. If individuals and teams formulate their own objectives and how to achieve them, they will have greater ownership of the objectives and accept greater responsibility for their achievement.

Objectives vary – some are quite specific, others more general. They also vary in terms of timescale and priority. At work, examples such as mission statements tend to be broad and long term, whereas many of us work with day-to-day objectives that are much more specific and short term.

What are the benefits of objective setting?

- Assists in the clarification of objectives
- Helps ensure a shared understanding of what has to be achieved

- Helps to improve communication processes in decision-making situations
- Develops skills in discriminating between different levels and types of objectives
- Assists in achieving consensus

Objective setting is closely linked to the planning process because without objectives you cannot plan. Consider the objectives that you are given at work and also the objectives that you set for others, and think about their place in the planning process.

Tools for the facilitator

The skills and techniques, such as communication skills, questioning techniques, debriefing, achieving consensus and objective setting, described earlier this week, are vital tools in the facilitator's tool box. However, there are a number of additional methods and tools that the facilitator can use, depending upon the situation, with both individuals and groups to identify and understand problems, set objectives, find solutions and achieve the task. The facilitator may require the following tools:

- Recording
- Brainstorming
- Ranking
- Affinity diagram
- A later list
- Reflecting back
- SWOT/PESTLE analysis
- Flowcharts

- Fishbone/Cause–Effect diagram
- Gantt chart
- Force field analysis

Recording

Accurately recording analysis, ideas, suggestions, discussions, summaries and any other issues is an important tool in helping individuals and groups. There are several ways in which information can be recorded: flip charts, white boards, electronic white boards, overhead projector slides and computers. The recording may be done by the facilitator or someone appointed from within the group.

Brainstorming

Brainstorming is a popular technique used for generating as many ideas as possible. Some ideas will be relevant and appropriate for the task; others will not. A facilitator can help improve the effectiveness of the brainstorming process and the eventual outcome by encouraging creative thinking and generation of ideas, by setting a timescale and controlling the time, and by recording the ideas on a flip chart or white board. Everyone needs to be encouraged to contribute as many ideas as possible with the shared understanding that there is to be no evaluation or criticism of individuals and their ideas. A useful approach is to ask all individuals by name for their contribution so that everyone participates. Building on other people's ideas is to be encouraged but the facilitator must end the session promptly when no more ideas are forthcoming.

Ranking

Ranking may come about as a result of brainstorming. It is a list of ideas or items that are sorted by priority. The priority is determined by discussion, debate and sometimes voting within the group. As a result of ranking, the number of items is often reduced. The facilitator has an important role in helping the group (or individual) to prioritise by asking questions and reflecting back. This ensures that the importance and feasibility of all suggestions are considered, discussed and debated. The facilitator can question the group or individual with regard to the decision, helping them to revisit and question certain decisions until they have reached a consensus about the ranking.

Affinity diagram

Affinity diagrams are used to organise quickly a large list of ideas. The ideas can be grouped in a number of different ways, by timescale, geographical location, resources, costs, etc. Again, the facilitator can help ensure that this process is more effective by questioning, prompting and using other communication techniques.

A later list
When groups and teams are discussing and debating issues, good ideas are often put forward that are not always directly relevant to the issue or relevant at that particular point in time. It is important to record such items and consider them later. If they are not recorded, they may well be forgotten. If they are discussed immediately then it is likely that the group will be distracted from its current task. The facilitator may be the most appropriate person to record these suggestions and certainly needs to remind the group of their importance at a later stage. Alternatively, the facilitator may suggest that someone from within the group be nominated to do this.

Reflecting back
Like a mirror, the facilitator can perform a useful function in reflecting back to individuals and groups, suggestions, ideas and proposals. This enables them to review their significance, evaluate proposals and revisit earlier events. Reflecting back questions and queries in a neutral way encourages the recipient to think further.

SWOT/PESTLE analysis
The analysis of an organisation's strengths, weaknesses, opportunities and threats is known as SWOT analysis. It is now widely understood, and used, and requires a systematic analysis of an organisation's internal strengths and weaknesses such as staff, buildings, money, products and services, together with external opportunities and threats such as competitors, economic changes and government. Whilst it is a simple technique, difficulties can sometimes be encountered as some strengths can also be listed as weaknesses (and vice versa), and the same is also

true of opportunities and threats. However, completing a SWOT analysis can provide considerable information about an organisation. Organisations do not exist in isolation and another common form of analysis is PESTLE analysis. This requires analysing the political, economic, social, technological, legal and environmental factors affecting an organisation. SWOT and PESTLE are often used together in order to comprehensively analyse an organisation and are useful for the facilitator who can assist individuals and teams in their analysis by providing a structure together with careful questioning, reflecting back, prompting etc.

Flowcharts

Flowcharts help describe and illustrate a process in a step-by-step sequence. They are useful because they depict visually what needs to be done in a logical and sequential way. A facilitator can make the flowcharts more effective by asking appropriate questions as they are being drawn. The facilitator can also summarise and reinforce what has been agreed, check for understanding and assist in ensuring that the flowcharts are accurate and useful.

Fishbone/cause–effect diagram

This is used to identify and organise information about possible causes of a problem and/or desired outcomes. The fish head represents the effect and the fish spine/bones represent the causes. It is another way of using diagrams to simplify a lot of information and assist with understanding. This is a tool that the facilitator can use both for their own benefit, or for the benefit of individuals, groups and teams. It helps to clarify situations, present information logically and assists understanding and decision-making.

Gantt chart

Gantt charts list the activities to be completed together with the name of the person responsible for the activity and the date of completion. They are a specific form of action planning. Again, the facilitator can assist groups in working more effectively by helping them to summarise, make decisions and move forward by action planning. The Gantt chart ensures that there is shared understanding of responsibilities and action together with key dates. It also provides a useful checklist for everyone of what was agreed and what needs to be done.

Force field analysis
Force field analysis is a particular form of analysis that highlights the forces for change and the forces for stability in a given situation. It is particularly useful for analysing and solving complex situations, especially those requiring change. Essentially, it is based on the assumption that any situation can be described as the meeting of two forces: the driving forces (prompting change) and the restraining forces (resisting change). To begin with, the forces must be identified and examined in terms of the amount of force they exert. Change can be brought about by either increasing the forces prompting change or by reducing the forces resisting change. Increasing the driving forces whilst at the same time weakening the resisting forces is an effective way of bringing about change.

Analysis is normally achieved through completion of a worksheet which encourages systematic analysis and decision-making, and enables complex problems to be broken down into smaller, more manageable and more understandable issues and tasks. The force field analysis worksheet comprises eight steps that logically follow on from one another. Those completing the worksheet are required to analyse the situation at each stage and provide sufficient detail to help them move on to the next stage. The worksheet includes the following steps:

Step 1.	The problem
Step 2a.	The present situation
Step 2b.	The desired situation
Step 3.	Restraining forces
Step 4.	Actions to reduce or eliminate
Step 5.	Driving forces
Step 6.	Actions to increase
Step 7a.	Steps towards solving problem
Step 7b.	Resources required
Step 8.	Sequence of steps

1 The problem

The problem needs to be identified and written down in a clear and simple way that everyone understands. Committing the problem to paper is an important first step as it helps to focus on it. With groups, discussing the problem at this stage helps determine and clarify what it is and assists with shared understanding.

2a The present situation

The current problem needs to be outlined in terms of context, the difficulties it is causing, the people involved and any other relevant information. Again, establishing these facts is an important part of the process as it aids understanding of the problem. The facilitator, by asking appropriate questions, can help individuals and groups with analysis and understanding.

2b The desired situation
Individuals and groups need to know what they want to achieve and what the desired situation is. Unless this is determined then it is very difficult to begin the necessary planning processes and take appropriate action. Without a desired outcome, resources and time are wasted. Again, the facilitator can assist individuals and groups in determining the desired situation by use of a range of tools and techniques.

3 Restraining forces
These are the forces that are resisting change. They need to be identified and examined in terms of the amount of force they exert. Individuals and groups need to identify and understand these forces as they prevent forward movement. To bring about change, these forces need to be reduced.

4 Actions to reduce or eliminate
Once the restraining forces have been identified, individuals and groups can consider how to reduce these forces or remove them altogether. A facilitator may work with small groups to brainstorm for possible ideas and suggestions.

5 Driving forces
These are the forces that are prompting change. They also need to be identified and examined in terms of the amount of force they exert. Individuals and groups need to identify them so that they can be used effectively. To bring about change, these forces need to be increased. Again, the facilitator may work with individuals and groups using a range of techniques to ensure identification and analysis of the driving forces.

6 Actions to increase
Once driving forces have been identified, consider how to increase their force and how to use them effectively. Facilitators can assist others in determining how to use driving forces to their advantage.

7a Steps towards solving problem
In this stage it is important to begin identifying the steps towards solving the problem. This is the very practical stage in terms of the action that needs to be taken. Questioning, brainstorming, summarising are some of the useful techniques a facilitator can use at this stage.

7b Resources required
Some resources will be required to bring about the identified changes. The resources may include money, people, equipment, particular skills, etc. These need to be accurately identified. Facilitation can help make this process more effective.

8 Sequence of steps
Finally, all the actions need to be ordered in a logical way, together with details of how the actions are to be achieved and by when. This provides an action plan that the individual or the team can use. The facilitator can assist in this final stage by ensuring that individuals and teams do not overlook any idea or action, and that all details are appropriately summarised and recorded.

Force field analysis is a useful tool for facilitators, individuals and groups/teams and can assist in resolving organisational problems and change, as well as helping individuals to change and develop.

Summary

Today we learnt all about facilitating individuals, objective setting and tools for the facilitator.

- There are many similarities between facilitating individuals and facilitating groups and teams
- Objective setting is important for facilitators, individuals and teams in order to evaluate success
- The facilitator needs to use a range of tools to be effective, including brainstorming, ranking, diagrams and charts
- Force field analysis is a specific analytical tool that is particularly useful in change situations

Pros and cons of facilitation

Today, we will examine some of the benefits and disadvantages of facilitation. We will also consider the manager as a facilitator and some of the difficulties associated with that role. In addition, we will examine what it is like to work with other facilitators, called co-facilitation.

- Benefits of facilitation
- Disadvantages of facilitation
- The manager as a facilitator
- Co-facilitation

There are many benefits in using facilitation in a work environment but it is not always the answer to the problem. Facilitation has some disadvantages and, therefore, we need to weigh up both the advantages and the disadvantages.

Benefits of facilitation

For those organisations that are moving towards empowerment, flexibility, improved performance and customer focus, facilitation is an important skill for managers, team leaders and other individuals. Adopting a facilitative style enables managers and team leaders to focus on getting the best out of individuals, groups and teams. Several different individuals and groups can enjoy the benefits of facilitation:

- The Facilitator
- The Team
- The Organisation
- The Individual
- The Customer

Benefits for the facilitator

Facilitators benefit from the process of facilitation as it provides them with the opportunity to learn about themselves, their skills and abilities, and about individuals and the way they work in groups and teams. Managers, team leaders and others who use facilitation can reduce their workload by delegation, freeing time for other projects and effective management. It reduces employee dependency, empowers the individual and increases involvement. Finally, facilitators can get involved with a variety of teams as well as overseeing projects and bringing to the employer's attention any major difficulties.

Benefits for the team

Facilitation can help team members take on greater responsibility for their own and the team's performance which, in turn, has benefits for the organisation. Collectively, the team can learn ways of dealing with problems, and opportunities for learning and development can be maximised. Newer team members can be accommodated more easily and more positively and team resources used more effectively. A facilitator can help teams have a greater sense of ownership and responsibility. They become more motivated and willing to share their ideas and, as a result, ideas and changes are more readily accepted. There is, therefore, an increased likelihood of the team reaching consensus and gaining commitment.

Benefits for the organisation

Facilitation has several benefits for the organisation in terms of working methods, staff motivation but, particularly, in improved productivity and quality of service. Those teams that work effectively are often prepared to share their ideas on good practice beyond the team, resulting in benefits for others. Facilitation can help reduce the dependency of employees and passes greater power and responsibility to the individual and teams. As well as increasing involvement and motivation, this can have the added benefit of reducing staff costs and increasing productivity. Teams are more likely to generate ideas, reach consensus and implement decisions that will succeed. The ability of individuals and teams to respond more flexibly to change, again has significant benefits for the organisation, through taking advantage of business opportunities and reducing the need to implement change. The opportunities for learning and development are increased, benefiting not only those individuals involved, but also the organisation as a whole. Finally, since facilitation requires trust and openness, it also helps develop these factors within an organisation, assisting in the formation of a more open and equal working culture with benefits for all.

Benefits for the individual
In general, facilitation empowers the individual, providing greater responsibility, a greater sense of ownership and increased involvement, although some individuals may disagree that an increase in responsibilities and the ability to make decisions are benefits. Facilitators provide support to individuals and help them to overcome difficulties. They can assist in preparing individuals for change and improving opportunities for learning and development. Most people find that working in an environment where there is increased openness, trust, autonomy and motivation is beneficial.

Benefits for the customer
Depending upon the type of organisation, facilitation can have positive outcomes for customers, such as an improvement in productivity and the quality of service. This may result in individuals and teams taking greater responsibility for problem-solving and addressing the needs of customers.

Disadvantages of facilitation

Whilst there are many benefits of facilitation, we have to admit there are also a number of disadvantages and those involved with facilitation should be aware of what they are:

- Facilitation will not work in every situation because sometimes direct instruction is more appropriate

- Facilitation may not be right for every group. Individuals/teams/employees must want to be facilitated and participate in the process
- Facilitation is not easy and will not be liked by everyone: some employees will prefer the traditional managerial approach of being told what to do
- The role of facilitator can be difficult and will not be a natural role for some employees; it requires training and development
- Facilitation can be time consuming and it may appear easier, quicker and more cost-effective to simply tell employees what to do
- The organisation must ensure an appropriate climate for facilitation with support mechanisms such as a 'no blame' culture or devolved responsibility

The manager as a facilitator

The manager as a facilitator can be a difficult role. Managers must remember that they are not task leaders; they are not there to contribute ideas and lead from the front. They should remain neutral, and help groups and individuals to achieve objectives and solve problems. In doing so, they need to be aware of the needs of all individuals and encourage solutions that ensure that those needs are fulfilled.

Why some managers find facilitation difficult
Facilitating groups and teams is very different from leading a group. Some managers find this difficult because their own individual needs are seen to take second place to those

of the group. The group/team is empowered and the manager may feel very disempowered. Many managers define their roles in terms of power, information and knowledge, and when this is passed to the team, they feel that their power and presence is reduced. In addition, some managers also feel uncomfortable in dealing with situations that require significant interpersonal skills and sensitivity, preferring hard facts and a hierarchical structure.

Facilitation involves asking and suggesting rather than telling and coercing and can cause some difficulties for some managers. Consider the differences between a manager who is an experienced facilitator and one who is inexperienced.

Experienced Facilitator	**Inexperienced Facilitator**
What do you think are the main issues regarding this problem?	*This is what I think are the issues . . .*
How can the problem be resolved?	*This is what we should do . . .*
Can you see any difficulties with that suggestion?	*I don't think it's a good idea. It will not work.*
Have you considered working with another team and sharing your knowledge and expertise?	*You can't do this is on your own. You don't have all the knowledge required.*
There are a number of very good ideas. Which ones are most likely to succeed and why?	*There are too many ideas. Which ones can we throw out?*
That's a good point. Can you make a note of it and discuss it later.	*That's not relevant, you're wasting time. Concentrate on the issue.*

Co-facilitation

Often you will work on your own in facilitating individuals and groups and that can be quite an isolating experience. It is possible for two or more facilitators to work very well together and benefit from the experience, although there are some basic requirements if this process is to be effective. This is called co-facilitation and can be defined as two or more facilitators working together at the same time or working together on the same event. There are several benefits of co-facilitation for facilitators, individuals and groups although, as we shall see, there are some disadvantages.

Successful co-facilitation

For co-facilitation to be successful there are a number of things that you need to be aware of and to have in place:

- Planning before facilitation begins
- Shared aims, objectives and outcomes
- Good communication between facilitators
- Development of relationships based on trust and honesty
- Establishment of ground rules for facilitators
- Agreement on roles, responsibilities and ways of working
- Recognition of power and variations in roles
- Awareness of personality and skills of other facilitators
- Regular review, feedback and support
- Willingness to learn, develop and improve

Before any facilitation events begin, there must be planning and a shared understanding of aims, objectives, outcomes and what is to be achieved. This requires good communication between facilitators. Whether you choose to work with another facilitator or whether because of organisational requirements there is no choice, it is important to develop effective working relationships. These relationships must be based on trust and honesty.

Ground rules need to be established both for effective working between facilitators as well as for working with groups to avoid confusion and conflicting messages for all who are involved. This particularly applies to how facilitators respond to groups and individuals. Facilitators need to agree on practical things such as roles and responsibilities, who is doing what, agreed methods of facilitating and joint ownership. Sometimes there can be difficulties associated with the distribution of power between facilitators and this must be established to ensure effective working arrangements.

The position regarding roles should also be clarified in terms of whether there is a team approach, an equal approach amongst individuals or whether the approach is that of learner and coach. Facilitators need to have an increased awareness of their own skills, the similarities and differences between their skills and those of other facilitators and an awareness of personality. No two facilitators will be identical, but they need to share core values, be able to recognise and deal with a range of issues and know what to do if something goes wrong or if there are problems with one of the facilitators. This requires regular review and evaluation of the facilitation process and of the facilitators. Facilitators need to provide feedback to groups and individuals when they are facilitating but they also need to give feedback to each other and receive feedback. In addition, they need to give and receive support and collectively have a desire to learn, develop and continually improve. There is, indeed, much to be gained for facilitators of co-facilitation:

- Support for facilitators and reduced stress
- Opportunity to learn, develop and receive feedback on performance
- Sharing of work, responsibilities and reduced individual risk
- Accurate assessment of behaviour, group dynamics, verbal and non-verbal messages
- Ability to facilitate sub-groups more effectively
- Improved recording of ideas, summaries etc. as one facilitator can facilitate and another can record
- Limitations of facilitators can be reduced
- Continuity if one facilitator is unable to facilitate

- Facilitators have available expertise to 'check out' queries, observations and ask for feedback on ideas
- Increased availability of experienced facilitators to deal with complex/challenging issues
- Increased wealth of potentially complementary skills increasing the pool of available skills

Co-facilitation also benefits individuals and groups through:

- Enhanced learning opportunities
- Expertise of more than one facilitator and variation in facilitator style
- Accurate assessment of behaviour, group dynamics, verbal and non-verbal messages and improved feedback
- More attention for sub-groups
- Improved recording of ideas, summaries etc as one facilitator can facilitate and another can record
- Continuity if one facilitator unable to facilitate
- Increased availability of experienced facilitators to deal with complex/challenging issues

However, despite the many advantages of co-facilitation, there is also the downside:

- Cost
- Conflict of style, differing approaches and methods, variation in pace of working and conflicting messages
- Potential differences and disagreements between facilitators
- Too much facilitation – it is only one technique/method
- Unequal distribution of work between facilitators
- Facilitators need to consider co-facilitator(s) and groups
- Group may believe they have a trainee facilitator or that one facilitator is weaker than the other
- Group may believe they are the problem and require more than one facilitator

Summary

Now we know about the benefits and disadvantages of facilitation, the manager as a facilitator and some of the difficulties associated with that role. We also understand co-facilitation and the requirements for this to be effective, together with some of the benefits and disadvantages.

- Facilitators, teams, organisations, individuals and customers can all benefit from facilitation
- Facilitation will not solve every individual and organisational problem – there are some disadvantages associated with facilitation
- Managers can use facilitation effectively as part of their job, although some managers will find facilitation a difficult technique to use
- Co-facilitation can be very useful and reduces isolation. Certain things have to be in place for it to be effective. It has a number of benefits but some disadvantages

Facilitation and you

Today, we will examine the future and what it means in terms of facilitation, particularly for you. A summary of facilitation will help you to evaluate your skills and develop them further. We will also consider how to devise an action plan so you can put into practice your facilitation skills.

- The future
- Facilitation and you
- Summary
- Evaluating your skills
- Action plan – putting it all into practice

The future

The world of work is constantly changing and with it, work roles. Managers, team leaders and employees have to work differently now from how they worked in the past; they will certainly have to work differently in the future. Employers are looking for improved performance, improved quality and greater organisational effectiveness. This potentially places pressure on team leaders and managers both to change personally and to bring about changes in their staff and the organisation. As a result, the emphasis within their roles is changing requiring different skills, including:

- Facilitating roles
- Effective communication, ability to motivate others and providing support
- Ability to develop effective relationships, openness, trust and fairness
- Excellent interpersonal skills, flexible, multi-skilled, co-ordination skills
- Ability to take decisions, solve problems, manage projects
- Ability to create opportunities for others to succeed
- Encouragement of staff to take control and make decisions
- Ability to develop individuals and teams
- Achievement of tasks and improved performance

Facilitation skills are seen as being one of the most important skills, together with communication skills and the ability to motivate others and provide support. Team leaders and managers still have as one of their key priorities the requirement to achieve tasks and improve performance. The additional skills required to enable this to happen are based on the ability to create opportunities for others to succeed, developing individuals and teams and encouraging staff to take control and make decisions.

Team leaders and managers, therefore, need to be able to develop effective relationships, develop an environment where there is openness, trust and fairness, and use a range of other interpersonal skills. They need to be flexible, multi-skilled, able to co-ordinate, able to solve problems and make decisions and, finally, able to manage projects in a constantly changing world. Facilitation and the skills associated with facilitation are particularly useful in achieving change.

Facilitation and you

Facilitation skills are useful for all individuals and form part of a tool box of skills to be used in a variety of situations. Facilitators need to be able to adapt and apply their skills to different situations and this requires planning and preparation for learning events, group sessions, meetings and other situations where facilitation will be used. If you are involved with facilitation, remember to:

- Ensure that facilitation is the most appropriate method to use in a particular situation
- Ensure that those who are facilitating have been trained and developed in facilitation skills
- Ensure that there are appropriate systems, structures and processes in place within the organisation to support facilitation
- Not use facilitation as the only method in an attempt to resolve all organisational problems and difficulties
- Be prepared to use facilitation with other skills such as coaching, mentoring and leadership
- Accept that not everyone will welcome facilitation and there may be some resistance to facilitation as a method

Facilitation within your organisation

Critically analyse how facilitation is used within your organisation. Try to observe an effective manager or colleague and analyse what do they do well in terms of facilitation. Ask yourself the following questions:

- What skills of facilitation does the person demonstrate?
  For example, using techniques such as, *What went wrong?*, *Talk me through it*, summarising, feedback, silence
- What can you learn from this person regarding facilitation?
- What are the important ground rules? (Getting to know each other, communication)

- What do teams need and how do they succeed? Team development, communication, planning, listening, action plan and dates
- When would facilitation be useful within your organisation?
- What changes would you need to make to structures and systems in order for facilitation to succeed?
- Who would you need to train and develop for facilitation to be successful?

If you want to use facilitation skills successfully, you need to plan how to use them within your job role. Having read this book, you should now have a greater understanding of the following:

- The role of facilitator and facilitation skills to achieve optimum results
- The use of facilitation tools including problem-solving tools
- The selection and use of facilitation methods and techniques to meet the needs of individuals and groups
- How to help resolve difficulties during group activities and deal with unhelpful behaviour
- The use of facilitation techniques as a means of helping group members improve their performance
- Facilitation in learning and development
- Effective debriefing and feedback
- Co-facilitation

Summary of successful facilitation

- Facilitation is about helping others help themselves to improve and accept responsibility
- Facilitators are like a conductor or a catalyst to speed up the process and make it easier
- Facilitation can be used in many different situations
- Learning and development is important in facilitation and is associated with action
- Facilitators need a range of different skills to be effective
- Many skills needed for facilitation are used in everyday situations, for example, communication, working with teams and personal skills such as tolerance and decision-making
- The role of a facilitator is to help other people develop, achieve things and improve their performance
- The style of a facilitator will vary as everyone is unique
- Communication techniques are vitally important for facilitation and include listening skills, questioning techniques and non-verbal communication
- Facilitators need to be able to observe individuals within groups and teams so they can understand group dynamics and what is happening
- Facilitators need to be able to help others understand what has happened during an event by debriefing them
- Facilitators need to be able to both give and receive feedback so that learning and improvement can occur for everyone

- Facilitators need to understand the stages of team development and their role in the process
- Effective facilitators need to prepare before a group session, work with a group and follow-up after the group session
- There are similarities between team and group events, and meetings, and many of the same principles can be applied to meetings
- Facilitators need to recognise conflict within groups and help groups resolve the conflict
- Groups and teams comprise many different individuals – facilitators need to understand different behaviours and have strategies for dealing with such difficulties
- Facilitators have an important role in helping groups and teams achieve consensus and group agreement
- There are many similarities between facilitating individuals and facilitating groups and teams
- Objective setting is important for facilitators, individuals and teams in order to evaluate success
- The facilitator needs to use a range of tools to be effective, including brainstorming, ranking, diagrams and charts
- Force field analysis is a specific analytical tool that is particularly useful in change situations
- Facilitators, teams, organisations, individuals and customers can all benefit from facilitation
- Facilitation will not solve every individual and organisational problem – there are some disadvantages associated with facilitation

- Managers can use facilitation effectively as part of their job, although some managers will find facilitation a difficult technique to use
- Co-facilitation can be very useful and reduces isolation. Certain things have to be in place for it to be effective. It has a number of benefits but some disadvantages
- The future requirements of team leaders and managers are changing
- Effective facilitators need to constantly review and evaluate their skills so that they can improve

Evaluating your skills

Like any skill, it is important to review and evaluate your facilitation skills. You need to consider those that you are competent in and those where there is room for improvement. You can use the summary of successful facilitation as a checklist and/or you can use the list below to evaluate your skills. The successful facilitator:

- Is well organised
- Makes people feel welcome and at ease
- Helps to establish ground rules for effective group working
- Shows enthusiasm
- Shows concern and understanding for individuals
- Uses tact and diplomacy in dealing with individuals
- Manages group and activities appropriately
- Encourages individuals to ask questions and participate

- Praises good work and corrects individual mistakes tactfully
- Relates well to other people
- Listens effectively and checks for understanding
- Provides feedback
- Encourages new ideas and experimentation
- Clearly defines aims and objectives with the group, with a plan showing how to achieve them
- Develops individuals and the team
- Helps individuals and teams to focus on achievement
- Assists in recording ideas and experiences

Evaluation should be a combination of self-analysis and feedback from others. You should ask for feedback from team members, colleagues or any other appropriate individual. There may be some variation in the skills you use depending upon whether you are using facilitation in learning and development or whether you are using facilitation to solve a problem. The following is an example of a form that you could give to other people for their feedback.

Facilitation skills	Excellent	Satisfactory	Room for improvement
Pre-meeting planning			
Helping people to get to know each other			
Establishment of ground rules			
Keeping people involved			
Listening effectively			
Managing time			
Recording			
Any other comments			

This is only a guide. You may wish to design your own checklist highlighting those skills that are most appropriate to the situation in which you are using facilitation.

Action plan

After reviewing and evaluating your facilitation skills, it is essential that you design an action plan so you can then practice and improve your skills. Remember to use experiential learning for yourself as a facilitator. Make your action plan as specific as possible.

- Things I do well
- Things I need to improve
- What I will do to ensure I improve
- What I will implement at work
- Future review and evaluation dates, for example, three months and six months
- Support and resources, for example, friends, colleagues, training courses
- How facilitation links to personal development plan and appraisal

Final thought

Successful Facilitation in a Week is only the beginning. There are many more weeks ahead and many opportunities to practice, develop and improve your facilitation skills. Take those opportunities so you can add effective facilitation skills to your personal tool box.

FACILITATION

Further *Successful Business in a Week* titles from Hodder & Stoughton and the Institute of Management all at £6.99

ISBN	Title	
0 340 71205 8	Appraisals in a Week	❐
0 340 70546 9	Assertiveness in a Week	❐
0 340 71197 3	Benchmarking in a Week	❐
0 340 57640 5	Budgeting in a Week	❐
0 340 74751 X	Bullying at Work in a Week	❐
0 340 72077 8	Business Growth in a Week	❐
0 340 70540 X	Business on the Internet in a Week	❐
0 340 71199 X	Business Plans in a Week	❐
0 340 59813 1	Business Writing in a Week	❐
0 340 71200 7	Communication at Work in a Week	❐
0 340 62032 3	Computing for Business in a Week	❐
0 340 73781 6	Consultancy in a Week	❐
0 340 74752 8	Credit Control in a Week	❐
0 340 71196 5	Customer Care in a Week	❐
0 340 70543 4	CVs in a Week	❐
0 340 72076 X	Dealing with Difficult People in a Week	❐
0 340 63154 6	Decision Making in a Week	❐
0 340 73762 X	Delegation in a Week	❐
0 340 62741 7	Direct Mail in a Week	❐
0 340 75336 6	E-commerce in a Week	❐
0 340 73048 X	E-mail in a Week	❐
0 340 64330 7	Empowerment in a Week	❐
0 340 66374 X	Environmental Management in a Week	❐
0 340 71192 2	Finance for Non-Financial Managers in a Week	❐
0 340 71189 2	Flexible Working in a Week	❐
0 340 67925 5	Fundraising and Sponsorship in a Week	❐
0 340 71204 X	Going Freelance in a Week	❐
0 340 65487 2	Human Resource Management in a Week	❐
0 340 74287 9	Information Overload in a Week	❐
0 340 74756 0	Interviewing in a Week	❐
0 340 71179 5	Intranets in a Week	❐
0 340 63152 X	Introducing Management in a Week	❐
0 340 71203 i	Introduction to Bookkeeping and Accounting in a Week	❐
0340 753374	Investors in People in a Week	❐
0 340 71202 3	Leadership in a Week	❐
0 340 71173 6	Management Gurus in a Week	❐
0 340 65503 8	Managing Change in a Week	❐
0 340 74757 9	Marketing in a Week	❐
0 340 47579 7	Marketing Plans in a Week	❐
0 340 57466 6	Market Research in a Week	❐
0 340 60894 3	Meetings in a Week	❐
0 340 74241 0	Memory Techniques in a Week	❐
0 340 61137 5	Mentoring in a Week	❐
0 340 71174 4	Mind Maps® in a Week	❐
0 340 73761 1	Motivation in a Week	❐
0 340 70545 0	Negotiating in a Week	❐
0 340 64341 2	Networking in a Week	❐
0 340 71123 X	Neuro-Linguistic Programming in a Week	❐
0 340 73812 X	Office Feng Shui in a Week	❐
0 340 72073 5	Personal Investment in a Week	❐
0 340 70541 8	Planning Your Own Career in a Week	❐
0 340 70544 2	Presentation in a Week	❐
0 340 71208 2	Process Management in a Week	❐
0 340 70539 6	Project Management in a Week	❐
0 340 64761 2	Problem Solving in a Week	❐
0 340 73780 8	Psychometric Testing in a Week	❐
0 340 56479 2	Public Relations in a Week	❐
0 340 71206 6	Purchasing in a Week	❐
0 340 73816 2	Recruitment in a Week	❐
0 340 71198 1	Report Writing in a Week	❐
0 340 70538 8	Selling in a Week	❐
0 340 67397 4	Selling on the Internet in a Week	❐
0 340 65504 6	Statistics in a Week	❐
0 340 72494 3	Strategy in a Week	❐
0 340 71201 5	Stress Management in a Week	❐
0 340 70542 6	Succeeding at Interviews in a Week	❐
0 340 71207 4	Teambuilding in a Week	❐
0 340 70547 7	Time Management in a Week	❐
0 340 71191 4	Total Quality Management in a Week	❐
0 340 75785 X	Tough Interview Questions in a Week	❐
0 340 71195 7	Training in a Week	❐
0 340 62102 8	VAT in a Week	❐
0 340 67905 0	Virtual Organisation in a Week	❐
0 340 70508 6	Web Sites in a Week	❐

All Hodder & Stoughton books are available from your local bookshop or can be ordered direct from the publisher. Just tick the titles you want and fill in the form below. Prices and availability subject to change without notice.

To: Hodder & Stoughton Ltd, Cash Sales Department, Bookpoint, 39 Milton Park, Abingdon, Oxon, OX14 4TD. If you have a credit card you may order by telephone – 01235 400414.
E-mail address: orders@bookpoint.co.uk
Please enclose a cheque or postal order made payable to Bookpoint Ltd to the value of the cover price and allow the following for postage and packaging:
UK & BFPO: £4.30 for one book; £6.30 for two books; £8.30 for three books.
OVERSEAS & EIRE: £4.80 for one book; £7.10 for 2 or 3 books (surface mail).

Name: ....

Address: ....

....

If you would prefer to pay by credit card, please complete:

Please debit my Visa/Mastercard/Diner's Card/American Express (delete as appropriate) card no:

❐ ❐ ❐ ❐ ❐ ❐ ❐ ❐ ❐ ❐ ❐ ❐ ❐ ❐ ❐ ❐

Signature .... Expiry Date ....